T0323735

# New Issues Poetry & Prose

| | |
|---|---|
| Editor | Herbert Scott |
| Copy Editor | Curtis VanDonkelaar |
| Managing Editor | Marianne Swierenga |
| Assistant to the Editor | Kim Kolbe |

New Issues Poetry & Prose
The College of Arts and Sciences
Western Michigan University
Kalamazoo, MI 49008

*An Inland Seas Poetry Book*

 Inland Seas poetry books are supported by a grant from
The Michigan Council for Arts and Cultural Affairs.

First Edition, 2006.

| | |
|---|---|
| ISBN-10 | 1-930974-66-3 (paperbound) |
| ISBN-13 | 978-1-930974-66-1 (paperbound) |

Library of Congress Cataloging-in-Publication Data:
McGath, Carrie
Small Murders/Carrie McGath
Library of Congress Control Number: 2006924617

| | |
|---|---|
| Art Director | Tricia Hennessy |
| Designer | Amy Elberling |
| Production Manager | Paul Sizer |
| | The Design Center, School of Art |
| | College of Fine Arts |
| | Western Michigan University |

# SMALL MURDERS

CARRIE McGATH

New Issues

---

WESTERN MICHIGAN UNIVERSITY

*for Herbert Scott*

# Contents

## Acknowledgments

*Poetry Motel:* "Escapism"

*Hiram Poetry Review:* "Murder Girl"

*Barrow Street:* "Little Girl with Blue Shoes"

*Vallum:* "Nights Marred Like Crickets in Metal Fan Blades"

Thanks to the above journals for including my work in their
publications.

Many thanks to my family, friends, professors and colleagues of
the past and present for their love and support.

Very special thanks to Marianne Swierenga for her friendship
and editorial guidance.

## Doll Crimes

I.

There was a small and clear plastic box
in an antique store on a haphazard corner.
In the store, various human things:
old license plates, frail postcards laid bare.
And there was a tiny room,
the ceiling low, the walls narrowing
as if the room were for children only,
as if for special cases and special consumption
of the images that plagued that tiny room:
a room of decaying dolls,
their eyes shot out by BB guns,
their faces cracking in sequence with the ticking of
grandfather clocks.
All victims of small murders.

Doll parts hung from a display:
brown hair, red hair, dishwater blonde hair,
feet, arms, legs, and heads with eyes,
eyes with eyelids that shuttered when touched.
These were exact dismemberments.
On the baby doll table sat a box.
A ten dollar tag lying idly by,
Inside the box: two baby doll teeth,
a small nursing bottle,
a tiny dustpan in 1950s blue.
Was this a chance meeting of misfit survivors?
Why in the middle of this table?
No guests watching? No one discussing?
I sat the gunshot doll at the table,
sitting an armless teddy bear beside her,
placing two jaundiced plastic arms before the bear
so he would have the illusion of arms.
I would return in a week.

II.

The room had been closed.
A grandfather clock kept time in the small doorway.
Yellow strips crossed the front of the room,
words laid in black:
*Caution. Do Not Enter. Caution.*
I knew what had happened: doll crime.
The owner sat behind a tall and wide counter,
a bulldog on his denimed lap. A smile for money.
I fingered the ten dollar bill in my pocket.
I fingered the chance to check on things.
*Are you looking for something?*
The bill in my pocket dampening.
My closed mouth asking repeatedly for the box.

## A Good Nympho Can Get a Lot of Guys Killed

Your breadth of knowledge about the remedies of pantylines
makes me feel that maybe even art is alive and well on pennies
a week, as alive as a blood-filled Homo sapiens sitting on the corner
collecting the spare change of strangers and succeeding
because of a knowledge of the deep such as panty lines.
Tell the guy shot over in apartment 605
the reasons why drives drove death to his hidden door
in his hidden house, rooms of so many obvious oversights.
I wish I had been there to hear a gun, smell the smoke,
resuscitate. But 605 was a one time thing for me. One night
after a subway ride, arteries of the city, bowels, caverns,
bone marrow, tubes jackknifed, cements carrying us
as if we were on the able back of a jackass on a dirt-covered road
somewhere. Not here. And didn't I call you a jackass
for not taking the love I gave you seriously?
And then I walked away wanting to cry but seeing the cool
absurdity of crying, so I didn't. Rage in my breasts, still feeling
teeth and fingernails needing clipping. So I give eighty-three cents
because it was in my coat pocket, close to my hip like a spleen,
a kidney. The streets are mean tonight, but still peaceful.
I think my peace has something to do with all the signs, lights.

## Fire Engine #45

When you make an appearance, look out.
Fire Engine Red, classic as a Slim '69 Corvette,
a true sign of deep anxiety, a power
only attainable through anxious ruin.
I have been ruined before, several times before,
several times you came along.
But now I use you, fire engine red, Maybelline 45,
to vandalize windshields that have jilted me.

My Fire Engine Red #45 came, saw, and conquered.
My little red wanderer, knowing the location of so much,
so much pain and the joy that barely follows it.

I need you now, tonight, today.
My anxieties so deep I shall need to employ a backhoe.
Part like the sea my lips, finally covered by thee.
All the windshields we have vandalized for our honor,
now a part of the part of my lips.

And you, always close,
rolling in the purse at my hip.
I love you, red vixen,
knight of my every fit.

An early death may suit you well.
You will be such a fallen angel, a fallen heroine.
Perhaps I shall donate you to the local mortuary.
An early death, immortality.
*You existential bitch,* I hear myself scream
from the barely-there security of bedsheets.
You pose before my vanity mirror
as I sit up in bed, duly petrified and interested
because I know you: a gun,
a gun that angrily aims its barrel between my lips.

## Murder Girl

In the first moments we're pregnant with the shock
of something gone wrong in the manicured,
pedicured street of a Midwestern suburb.
We are all focused on this girl, maybe seventeen,
lying on the pavement, mutilated,
likely raped, her hot pink panties just
above her knees, her white miniskirt rolled up,
a torn black lace bra surrounding small breasts
—underwire for lift and confidence.
All of this blossomed girlhood exposed
beneath a ripped white T-shirt.
Here is a tattoo near her navel,
a postal stamp with a calla lily inked into its center.
I can imagine her bitching about the pain
of the needle to her closest girlfriend.
I can imagine her hiding it from her mother.
Her body is looking to us more and more like a mangled sheet
beneath a painter's feet, red specks everywhere,
some darker than others. Blood type. DNA.
A lot of blood, but not the volume of blood
we would expect from her mangled body.
There must have been more.
We form a circle around her
as the air around us feels like rain approaching.
Our bodies in working order above her do not help.
She lies there as our darkest dream.
Her legs from the knees down shoved inside the street sewer,
left to hang. We imagine sewer rats nibbling
on what I suspect to be hot pink polished toenails.
Her clogs are discarded near each of her ears,
her fishnet stockings are ripped and left at her waist,
pieces here and there about her thighs and knees.
*Has anyone called the police?* asks a voice.

*Yes,* answers a woman decked out in Adidas
as she rolls her baby's stroller back and forth
to stop the cooing that seems both right and inappropriate.
Two men approach and add themselves to the circle,
both in black suits with red neckties.
They cross their hearts lazily with gold-ringed fingers: *Holy moly.*
Another man comes down from his telephone pole.
*Do you think she was a hooker?*
We all want to touch her,
to pull her from the sewer at the very least,
to try to comfort her dead body with hands.
Our reason catches our hands reaching out for her,
our reason tells us: *Never touch a crime scene.*
One of the "holy moly" men lights a cigarette,
the Adidas mother asking: *Hey, can I have one of those?*
We stand over this murdered girl, two now smoking,
this girl, looking more and more like a fashion shoot
I saw in *Soma* magazine,
a magazine I bought under a sign: *Women's Interest.*
A layout: "Murder Girl Fashion."
The police arrive, the detectives to disperse the bodies.
I'll leave as soon as her unnibbled hot pink toenails
are revealed to us and to the storm's coming air
that never stops surrounding us.

## Woman in the Glovebox of Henry's Taxi

The Virgin's arms are reaching for a tiny city in Barbados,
a city situated right below her left hand.
I ask her if she was ousted by the dashboard
or ousted by Henry, then put into the glovebox.
Henry speaks to Priscilla the prostitute, who is in the backseat,
about her allergies to shellfish and says
    she should really try imitation crab.
I ask the Virgin again why she was ousted.
She doesn't want to talk about it.
She is silent as an ice cube and feels as cold,
ghost-cold. I feel the coldness of the glovebox
as I enter beside her. Henry and Priscilla, chatter on.
The Virgin doesn't care to wonder why Henry ousted her.
And now I am in the glovebox with her and Henry seems pleased,
though indifferent to my whereabouts, *our* whereabouts.
Why is he pleased I sit in here with the Virgin,
the Virgin who is even more silent now, like a doorstep?
Last week I ate all of his shrimp.
I thought they were for everyone,
even me, dressed in my overcoat perusing the refrigerator
looking for something valuable I may have left there.

The Virgin knocks on my head:
*My suction cup just does not suction anymore. It hasn't since autumn.*
I am no longer in the mood to talk.
I just want to make the best of a bad situation.
But she keeps on in a voice I would not expect of the Virgin,
a voice that sounds as if it were running through a wrapping paper tube:
*I think that when the weather got cooler, the suction didn't work anymore.*
My heels and toes sleep and are comfortable in their position.
My head starts to ache, thanks to my nose fixing on the smell
of taxi breath coming in from under the hood.
I give the Virgin my plastic barrette to talk to.

Why is the Virgin's voice so deep?
Is she lost in the very tube that creates her voice?
She seems to be wanting to occupy and be occupied.
Looking at my plastic barrette, the Virgin inquires as to why it exists,
why I use it, says my long hair looks better without it.
I knew then that I would be content in the glovebox
if I were alone.

*Did you stop working, too?*
She does not know I am a human woman, Henry's woman.
I look at her with my solid blue eyes,
my eyes like baby blue construction paper
sitting in my sockets, laden with rubber cement.

I wonder where Henry goes in his life now.
Does he now notice how neat and small I have become to him?
I am a convenience, even a luxury, an ordinary object.
A compact. I am a compact now,
in this glovebox, in this still-folded position.
From the waist up I am a mirror. My lap is the hollow
where powder and a powder puff would go.
My legs fold under me, both functional and decorative,
make up a ribbed design for better grip.

Henry is teaching me a lesson. Maybe it's a lesson
about not eating shrimp from the refrigerator—
not to eat shrimp while I stand in the kitchen in an overcoat,
thinking of the shrimp there on a plate and not of him.
They look at me for help, for life again
their curvatures like fetuses straining
into development and new sets of lives.
I ate them. I just didn't think.
And now Henry is pleased I am in the glovebox of his taxi.

The dashboard Virgin reads the Barbados map
to my barrette and enjoys herself,
while Henry's voice sounds something like pomegranate seeds
arranged into crowds.

## Admonishment

I aim to be your first brunette.
The pigs at the trough below the kitchen window
wake you early.

There's a first time for everything.
The blistering truth of mud: filth
fills me again, senses of life

begin to depart over the rims.
I was always the sick one, till now.
The heavy breath of you in that room

makes me want to walk away,
back to the woman I left in Tallahassee.
But I aim to be the honorable

one in this and all things now.
The view from our roof is fetching.
And it fetches me now,

this night that feels lighter than others.
I fear the end is pursuing me,
not you. And I will go with it.

The pigs need more, always need more.
And I am called through them again
to you, my blonde heavy-breather.

A woman in Winn Dixie said I looked
like her red-headed cousin, ten years dead.
I feed the mud as I feed the pigs.

So much is a cycle, cycles and circles,
cyclical contraptions I cannot yet begin
to administer, to allow to happen in my house.

# Escapism

You, on my pillow,
while I look at Kurt Seligmann's *Will o' the Wisp:*
four arms coming from a vase.
You, escape my grasp.
You, a will o' the wisp,
Asleep in my twin bed,
the bed I escape to when you escape me,
the bed of my childhood, the bed where I lost it all:
my taxes, my calculator, my girlhood.
You, oblivious to me,
will o' the wisp, the complete escape.
All four hands grasping
for something. Difficult but convenient escapes.

Days between us pass in slow droves,
and you in constant, quiet escape, right before my eyes.
Your methadone clinic demons just far enough away,
but never quite far enough. We grapple blindly
for the things others can see, even in the kitchen sink,
where they reluctantly hover after meals, cleaning up.
You, my will o' the wisp,
are always relaxing, always escaping
the porcelain hunger of sinks.

## Daylight Savings

I have become a bathtub, scum
stubborn, I am a bird born naked and blind.
I have lost my way. What would the past say

if it had seen all of this? I try to recover
from drugs I have never administered,
and feel a motivation to simply sip

things from cups, cans, and bottles.
I find no comfort in comfort foods.
In an old photo I see you guys smoking

cigars without me in a diner, discussing
someone's legs: curvy but hairy,
and I feel I am the loneliest girl in the time zone.

Me and my convictions lie down together,
I guess in sin, or in simple and complete desperation,
as I love a real man raw and wonder

how he will make it through life like this.
*You wear me down,* he says through closed eyelids
and throbbing headaches.

There is a pile of eggshells somewhere close
from which I hatched years ago.

# Having Hans Bellmer's Baby

When my water broke, I was standing over Hans
as he pounded nails through the thigh of his latest doll creation.
I had never gotten around to telling Hans our lovemaking had taken,
and all he thought these months was that I had gained some weight.
I was silent when my water broke, not really aware of my own body.
I watched my uterine fluids run down the bare back of Hans.
I watched the doll he was gently nailing together:
her face, newly melted and molded, was frightened by me.
She seemed to know what was happening in my body.
She looked at me, her first vision after her rebirth
out of the odd ends of mannequins,
and I was a vision of some ball-bellied, ugly angel.
Her face, a slowly sunken pomegranate
in some forgotten refrigerator.
Then Hans looked up at me,
noticing that he and his new doll were puddles:
water dripping down my Hans's spine,
water in the doll's surprised and open eyes,
in the slick ridge between her pouty plastic lips.

I drove myself to the hospital after running
    from the screaming of Hans.
I knew he wanted only dolls, not humans
but my body must have had other ideas.
The labor was numbness.
I could think only of the silence of houses.
She came from me without a sound,
and the doctor held her upside down,
like fresh catch off a pier.
My daughter, new as a kitten,
her eyes shut tight like window blinds.
Her subsequent cries I could even taste,
her lips so perfectly round they seemed to be stamped onto her face.

## Surgery: A Reluctant Love Poem

Now that surgery goes on just under my nose,
it really no longer fascinates me.
The tools are no longer a mystery,
their curvatures and cold temperatures
are instead predictable. The movement
of surgery, the same slow motion.
The tools are always laid out
in alphabetical order when *you* lay them out.
When I lay out the tools, I lay them out by preference.
I am a fan of scalpels.
Petri dishes await my specimens.
Today, those specimens are from my lover,
from *you,* lover. An eyelash from your left eye and one from your right.
I want to see the differences,
if there are differences, between them.
I struggle with my microscope days later,
after the eyelashes have had the chance to forget,
in a petri dish, being a part of your eyes,
after they have stopped their constant crying for you
late in the night. Your eyes like phantoms to them.
And as I struggle with my microscope
and the eyelashes and the slide,
you stand at the bathroom sink combing your hair,
your DNA falling to the porcelain
to be left there until water washes it
and the drain sucks it away.
One less thing to examine, to dissect.
Your eyelashes were indeed different, different in temperament.
The left eyelash, laid-back. The right, high-strung, still missing your eye.
I guess that is why I sleep near the right of you;
I am similar to the right side of you.

## Rat-Tailed Radishes

I knew a certain woman once
when I worked with vegetables.
Days when I would enjoy the perfume of manure
lining vegetable bodices: carrots like number two pencils,
pears like corseted ladies in chewed-up wicker.
This woman wanted to rid the earth of the small fears:
rats, bats, spiders, insects.
She had killed many rats,
memorizing their dying.
But one can never find women like that again,
after daily dealings with them.
I quit the market long ago.

Walking into my kitchen
I find a hummingbird on the counter,
puncturing the radishes I had left there.
Why had I left them on the counter?
Why was a hummingbird in my kitchen,
feasting on my radishes?
How did she puncture the hard radish skin?
Why did she hum, as she feasted, as my refrigerator hums,
reminding me that I should have put my radishes in there?
I open the window and ask her to leave.
She looks up at me,
her breast dyed radish red.

## Little Girl with Blue Shoes

Walking through the park,
I see a little girl with blue shoes.
The shoes shine with the day and sport straps
across the top of her little feet like worms painted in oils.
The little girl with blue shoes stands on a cement path.
Walking up to her I see her body through her white blouse,
a body where the interiors are hidden only
by the two straps holding up her blue corduroy jumper.
I see her lungs, her fragile ribcage giving her body its shape,
its absolute perfection.
The blouse seems cotton, but the light from her body
makes the blouse a veil, protecting her heart from the wind.
Kneeling down, I watch her eyes refuse to follow me,
and I wonder if I should even speak.
*What's your name?*
The silence that follows my question, like a shriek in a cave.
Does she answer me through the ceased barking of dogs,
through the ceased movement of the leaves in the trees?
Her eyes move into mine and I feel her eyes inside my eyes,
our vitreous humors mix like batter with metal whisks.
I can tell now she sees what I have seen today:
the general misunderstandings of loneliness.
The understanding between us to help one another
with the locks, the trapdoors, our thoughts
that do not stop spinning for anything,
not even the scary noise of sirens, screeching tires.
We stand together, in the park, on the path's cement.
So much seems to be happening under us,
so much happening in our vitreous humors.
Any thoughts I had before have left me.
Leaving me behind like an outdated specimen
in a vial labeled with an indecipherable classification.

## Window-Shopping

Doctor, the woman in your window display looks so calm.
You gave her three sets of breasts,
ordered large to small.
And I see her breathing, the three sets of breasts
like the breathing skins of approaching caterpillars.
Could you give *me* the complication of three sets of breasts?
Use my teeth if you need them, to cut me open.
When you are finished, tie me together with surgeon's knots.
Hold the string as your cold red fingers pull the tight knots through me.

The street outside your window is of cobblestone.
I stand here, studying them.
Dear surgeon, dash away my large nose with these stones,
use them as leveling blocks to make my sagging perky again.
These stones align your street, doctor, why not use them
to make new pieces of me, or reconstruct what I have already?

Your building looks like bone marrow:
yellowing and darkening, marbleizing.
Did I walk into your bones when I walked through your door?
Do you like the dress I am wearing for you?
I have walked into your bones' marrow after ringing your bell
to let you know I have come to have some work done.
When you are finished with me, I want to be priceless,
as priceless as a working heart, a functioning kidney.

Could you give me four sets of wings?
I know you can. I have the highest confidence in your work.
Breasts are not much different from wings:
both allow one to float in water, in air.
Knot like knuckles.

I am a happy woman of knots now.
I possess bellies and wings and a small nose upon a thin, teardrop face.
You shaped me after your favorite thing, a wine bottle.
And I am forever in your room of beauty,
sometimes behind glass.
And my body thanks you for making me all in one,
thanks you for a winged freedom
and the prison I have become.

## In Wait

Now even the belly dancers are out of a job,
so I suppose I am glad I am not full of glee today.
The world has opened, inviting such has–beens as ourselves,
has–beens waiting for something to happen
—something simple, nuclear, or just plain mundane.
I sit and try to figure out what to do
—go to Aries Pub, read Lorca, go shopping.
Nothing seems to be winning.
Nothing wins me over
as you sit to the left of me
as I write our secrets in meager manners called words.
You ask me what you can do for me
as I write the words: *What can you do for me?*
But I play the marty r so well
I hate for it all to stop and I wonder when it will all stop
without permissions, my permissions in particular.
Art museums stand in wait for something.
Centuries pass, curses yet unlifted.
I drizzle my bed with anisette and lie down.
Emotion suddenly causes something in the way of aromas.

I wait on you hand and foot, but it's okay.
No one would understand our arrangement.

## Finding Frida Kahlo in My Chest of Drawers

Peering into my sock drawer, I see a woman.
She is rolled and folded, between my socks.
The odd thing, though, is that she has placed herself
    in the color scheme: nothing
in my color-coded sock drawer is in the least compromised.
I actually like the look she brings to the drawer:
the reds and golds of her dress complementing
    the reds and golds of my argyles.
Her black hair bun stares up at me,
the giant eye of an ant catching the morning light.
Her clothing, its tapestry, telling me a story of a trial.
Her head swings up towards me to reveal her face,
a truly beautiful contraption.
Her eyebrows, the only thing speaking and animated.
I want to invite her to have coffee with me,
a morning talk perhaps.
She stands up quickly then, noiseless,
jumps from the drawer and walks away.
I follow her closely,
asking her if she wants coffee,
maybe some breakfast.
She stops and sits politely at the café table.
I pour and bring cream and sugar.
She sips the coffee black and takes a cigarette.
*Your dress, I understand the story.*
I wonder if she chose my sock drawer
because she thought I would not recognize her.
I will not mention I know who she is.
I say it again, *I understand the story.*
She is as quiet as the large ant stuck in the lacy tablecloth,
and oddly calculating in her glare as the blind eye of a cicada.

Days later, I get out of the shower to find her smoking on my toilet.
I thought she had left me.
I even dismissed her as an apparition, a figment.
But now she sits on my toilet waiting for me,

handing me my towel.
She gets up and walks away,
the cigarette smoke following her like a mist of fruit flies.
I find her in my living room, waiting with tea and cleaned ashtrays.
Maybe now she wants to talk about it.
Maybe now she sees us both lost in the same miniature dollhouse,
waiting on men who only find us
when they grasp for the comforts of the necessary in the dark.
Frida's in the shower now,
washing away leftover lint from her black hair.
I lie upon her tapestried dress and watch the action there:
the moderate, blood-like movement of the embroidered lines,
lines creating a story
of those wronged in dark places.
I seep slowly into the dress and become part of the embroidery.
I feel odd but content there,
odd because I am led along eerie paths;
content because I recognize the scenario of obligations.
But now I hear voices in the world above me
and I have been scooped up by large, commanding hands
that shake and wring me dry.
This is not Frida, but someone else.
I still hear the faint sounds of a running shower.
I am dropped onto the floor then,
my body now in many knots.
The door shuts like a subtle command.

## Erotic Neurotic

You may as well be a hit man entering my kitchen at 3 A.M.
for an apple from the crisper drawer. I lay sleeping,

in sheets simply riddled with you.
I bet there is a silencer somewhere, among your belongings.

The black leather gloves, I have indeed seen, packed away
with sweaters and sweatshirts, a wool jacket.

Sitting stoic isn't so much your strong suit, but
lying stoic is—neck bent uncomfortably, the pillow acting

more as a hindrance than a comfort.
I watch you more than you would ever think, and

and it concerns me, that I watch you so intently, so enthralled;
I guess you are my personal entertainment, a novel I am half through,

a song, or a television show blaring. But I seek you, I think.
I do not watch you as much as I seek you. Then I will fold you away

for later consumption in bed, in the dark, as you lay beside me,
and I think and examine, and I envy your ability to sleep so soundly

so very quickly. But in those dark hours, you steal away for apples,
silencers, rifles, and milk in a kitchen I thought I knew so well.

# Two Paintings by Salvador Dali

I.

Perhaps you saw fertilic hope in the supple purity of the fruit dish,
the sadness of the people as harbingers of the horizon's hope.
But what did you think, dear miser of my innards,
    about the noose-like rope?
The rope that is thrown off to the side,
almost falling out of the landscape,
the rope that causes a fear in me,
so that I choose a barrenness instead.

II.

The woman in *Female Figure with Head of Flowers* is hopeful,
and in that landscape, no discernible ropes,
yet no hope because there is no discernible horizon.
She is a flower-head, beautiful with oddities,
fruitful in the uterine sack,
the pointed, ready-to-eat breasts.
A barely discernible man bows to her,
a barely discernible woman, almost a white paint splash,
dances in celebration very much behind her.

## "... and sucks like octopi on my tongue"

*from "The Love Plant" by Anne Sexton*

And where should I take that delightful line?
I know we're ready to go,
ready for the big step to the door and for the world
that came before that door.
I have bundled up the line in mittens and scarves,
and bundled myself as well.
Swaddled.
The line and I are swaddled from the cold,
for the cold outside that door
outside of which is the world that came well before
that door.
I have the line on a leash,
the leash I usually wrap like a balloon's strap
around my son's wrist.
But where should I take this line?
Where shall we go to wine and dine?
To be honest, I feel something
different on my tongue, a burning from hot tea.
I feel like a kidnapper.
I feel the least I could do would be to call up Anne
and tell her, warn her of a ransom,
what any self-respecting kidnapper would do.
How can there be so many kidnappers in the world?
I hardly think it is worth the trouble.
You are getting antsy, line.
You are wondering and quivering about what I am going to do
with or without you.
Your Os in OctOpi are morbid eyes
and you may kill me with surprise.
I think you want to pull really hard on this leash
and give me the surprise of palpitations.

Now I know where this line is to go.
It reminds me of a place in a cubbyhole of me.
A place down past my liver and spleen.
So here we go out of that door
and into the world that came before
to reach that place that is past it all,
past the grin on the cusp of my face.
The street that is marked with a bookmark:
Sheridan Avenue, the place where a man's voice
would speak and creep down my neck, into my dress.
It is a dark place, line, a cubbyhole in me.
Yes, line, don't be scared.
There is one man I hope to see
who sucks like octopi on my tongue.
He is the one.
The man with the felt hat on.
The hat he wears so that I will be able to know him,
even when he is dead.
I remember him so sweetly and well,
although he damned me to hell.
He is just inside the door of my mouth
*and sucks like octopi on my tongue,*
*and sucks like octopi on my tongue.*

## To Sleep and Constellation Determinations

I must be naked, and I will need a partner
to connect the dots around my buttocks and back.
The unreachables. I have struggled.
But you, so tired tonight. But my hope
is that you will help me anyway. I struggle
in asking you now if you think this is crazy
because I know you will think so, but say
nothing to me about craziness, craziness
being a sore spot, subject, as sore as a new pimple.
As sore as those sore spots of our past,
the soreness of warm drugs curdling
when it touches cold bloods that run
through all of us, the bloods that try, struggle
so heartfully to be truly warm, but then
we realize, that's why drugs exist, why
passion and addiction, why love and hate
exists within us like breath, exists in us like
veins and sinews we will live without knowing
they even exist in us. We only know the existence
of that which we administer
into ourselves on cold, dark nights in the world—
the Midwest, Europe, the Southwest, and Asia.
Something within us has yet to be awakened in many cases.
We do not know the feeling of so many things,
die trying to reach them. Catastrophe.
When reaching for our drink from long distances,
catastrophe. Spillage and anger, even some rage
and sadness in manifestations we have not yet seen in her.
She waits on the bus. I wait on something,
sadness comes because I wait but I do not know
what it is I am waiting for with this bated breath.
I wait for you to connect the dots, see what constellation
my body has composed, unknown to me.
The formation that formed while I went on with it,

all of it, clueless to the stars and the sadness of life.
I know less now than ever, and I am not a part
of something missing parts. The caveat of life
is life in the long days we live, never listening.

## The Reversible Axis

*for Hans Bellmer*

Your navel spoke volumes as you slept tonight.
Late getting to bed, I had this opportunity
of truly listening. I had a strong feeling
no one had heard it speak before tonight.

The headlights driving by our window, shadows
spliced like paper in a rage seen rarely on earth.
I feel the cold of the moon now as I sit
listening intently. And I hear a friend of yours

speaking through you. There has been shit
going on tonight I know nothing about,
but I move on triumphantly in the knowledge
of myself becoming the other: my feet

becoming hands reaching out from pant legs.
I tremble as I hear your voice return.
The navel works its magic, thoughts palpable
by means of words, weapons of true destruction

tonight in this room of this world. The tea kettle
across the hall sounds again as if it is an alarm,
a bomb warning us to safety of isolation,
lobotomy lunch, iliacs barely covered with French lace.

## Heroin Heart

I.

You, a secret in a sternum,
in the atrium, the corner shadows of an atrium.
My ear, my right ear, resting on your chest.
You had been gone so long.
But now, here you are.
I am truly a pesky creature hovering.
Does that she still prowl your heart?
Still pump in there, in the beats I hear with a right ear
that does not really believe what it is hearing.
Is this the reason for the slow, melodic beats
beating in the drum of my ear?
It has been years since that she was in your veins.
So much depends on the composure of so many things,
so much probably lingers.
Residues. Residual effects.
Too much passion, here, must slow
to a crawl across a room a thousand miles long,
thousands deep. Too many river regions here
to ever even begin explorations.
Will anything ever be known?
Do I share your heart with ground poppies
of thousands and thousands of nights ago?
Should I stay here hearing?
Shall I move, or completely go?

If ever your heart is extracted,
will its surfaces be shaved away and examined,
all its parts laid completely, so very bare?
Examined like newly discovered sea urchins:
> *What's there? What is it?*
> *A face of a sad woman, tar, that drug?*
> *Lover, where have you been all your life?*

Your heart, its contents and membranes will indeed baffle.
But you will be able to be put back together in the end,
put back right, your heart back in, intact.
As if nothing has ever ever happened,
ever ever plagued you away from so much.

II.

After I love you, your lips are as cold as frostbitten fingers,
like my fingers after I bury them, bare, in snow drifts for hours,
hoping the snow will become the sands of an Atlantic beach.
Why does so much misery exist
when I hear life should be nothing short of pure bliss?
I have been happy here, a few times, a handful.

## The Meeting

We were tamed by the subversive look of one another
back then in the dark, sitting there, all things considered,
as the sad ones. We wanted to be each other's inconvenience,
a problem of resolute love. And the couch that counts your coins
is always dirty to you. The clinical part of us is what unnerves,
the thing that keeps doubts lagging, while my lungs deepen
and your blood thins into the nothing I fear will finally
overtake us completely. And there is always the front door
tempting me in or out, or another in or out, tempting me to wait.
I stand there at the whitewashed wood holding an envelope
full of fear. The letter inside needed to be written,
just as it needed never to be sent. And the silence of another
human being on this earth distracts me from everything.
You sleep while I stand and I believe what you say in sleep.
You are a quarter of your way to finally waking.

## You Are a Rifle in my Closet

You are a rifle in my closet, kept there until intruded upon.
You will always be there in dark recesses,
closed in by grainy wood and metal hinges.
All I ever wanted: you with a top hat
full of emotions manufactured only for me.
But there you are now as I work miles away, in another cubicle,
leaning against a cold white wall on the inside
as I am elsewhere thinking of you just as constantly.
I have used you before, even pondered what you could do
for me in a night, after an afternoon of thinking, doing
what I think I may want to do if I am not getting
the hang of myself, if you and I still exist in separations.
The middle of the night, as difficult as a heart attack.
Who wants the neighbors to see the lights, hear the sirens
in the middle of the night? All that ruckus just for you and me.

Tonight you smoke in there. I can smell the odd odor.
I begin smoking too, rooms away, to feel closer.
But something always keeps the trigger locked and you
on the other side of me. Trigger, out of order, you say softly.
And you continue talking a few more moments,
telling me you hope I never need to kill a rabbit for dinner,
a raccoon for getting into things, for being too close.
Is there ever a good time for you?
Never is a good time you say.
So I sit still, rooms away, mourning something,
something like the impossibility of triggers, dumb luck.

## Entourage

They have been quick to judge me as I sit readily waiting
for someone else. The challenge has presented
itself slowly but deliberately as confounded children scream
for me. In a station where trains occasionally run I see you,

and the minutes fill the hour quick and large. I see the methods,
theirs and yours as the palpable air becomes a burlap bag,
a potato sack for the racing of hearts and rates unsurpassed
by nothing and no one. You appear as if by visions, my entourage

knowing the secrets I try to hide slowly in my brain stem.
Brain stem, stem of brain where I possess the deepest of files,
documents behind locks but quickly jimmied like suburban doors.

# The Plastic Peeping Tom in the Mannequin Warehouse

He doesn't have a penis, molded plastic or otherwise,
so it is hard for me to see his motivations.
Nor does he have arms with which to search for motivations.

Watching him leer at three armless mannequin women,
dressed only in lacy primrose panties,
I can imagine where his satisfied grin comes from.

Six breasts of plastic, each female mannequin possessing a pair,
six tilted teepees seemingly screaming for either attention
    or invisibility.
I cannot know which. Do they seem comfortable in his gaze?

Yes, a peeping tom in the department store warehouse,
just off the dressing room of lingerie and boys' clothing.
He looks at the blondes, and the blondes put smiles on.

They are enjoying something he gives. The blondes,
members of some odd blonde mannequin clique.
The brunette is only a torso on a table in the corner.

And now we come face to face, peeping tom.
I am to clean you up and dress you for the floor.
I am, also, to find your arms and attach them as seamlessly

as possible. But the girls will not be coming with you.
The girls are not needed in lingerie, not completely.
In lingerie, torsos have taken the place of full-bodied mannequins,

plastic torsos that show off the bras, panties
much more efficiently and without the distraction of plastic eyes
in inhuman colors. No eyes or smiles will be there to satisfy you.

So I am sorry, peeping tom, but you will be leaving them.
I have already found your arms, and it will take only a moment
to put them back into your sockets so that they can display a bookbag

for the back-to-school display in the red-and-orange-colored
    boys' department.
I am sorry to be doing this, but it is my duty tonight,
tonight in the after-hours glaze of midnight.

The perfumes from the cosmetics girls hustling out to their cars,
still loom and seem to be the music in the air to which we dance.
Yes, you and I are dancing as I put your little plastic body
    on a platform.

## Door-to-Door

The Surrealists stand outside my door begging for words.
I refuse them, like Jehovah's Witnesses, but watch them.
I do not want them to go away.
They seem to be making themselves comfortable,
lighting cigarettes, sipping from flasks and Thermoses.
They have books in their laps. They are scratching their heads.
I begin to suspect my mean neighbor next door
told them I was the woman they were looking for,
the woman they hoped would be a match for Nadja.
They may think I am the one to decode
the strange, the automatic phenomenon of America.
But perhaps they're too late.
I am on Prozac now.
Maybe my muse-like abilities went with the blood tests,
the vials of my identity the doctor needed
*to know what is going on in there.*
The men, at least seven of them, were still outside at midnight.
It was getting colder and darker in the cold and dark.
I wanted to let them in for warmth and light,
but I knew I would have to let everyone in—
every surrealist, salesman, Jehovah's Witness.
So I slip them what they wanted from me:
words on the backs of cicadas,
cicadas from my collection, who would fly out to them blindly,
words attached to their backs by pearls of rubber cement.
The Surrealists did not see the words at first.
But soon the cicadas, blind and dying,
flying into their faces or landing at their feet.
revealed the glued words on their little backs,
tiny last wishes, last words:
*the, big, fast, lascivious, barnacle, run, be.*
The Surrealists grabbed the words, crawling
on all fours across one another fighting over words, meanings,

and they looked like children now, children fumbling
over candy thrown from a fire truck in a parade,
as discarded cicadas lie on the fake grass carpet
like saints fallen, some twitching, some motionless and humming.

# My Guardian Angel Swallows Her Corsets and My Garter Belts

My guardian angel is an octopus,
and she has come to me out of boredom.
She is wearing a corset, tied tight,
but she looks good in that corset,
and the pain and difficulty is little enough to pay
for her beauty.
She enters my bedroom and opens the lingerie closet.
She pokes through the closet with her eight arms,
making wet sounds in an odd rhythm.
Removing her corset, she begins to talk to me
about how her husband has abused her for years
and had an affair with a spadefish.
Her skin is marked like a scored cake.
She seems grief-stricken.
Her back resembles broken seashells.
She is comprised of hardships,
and has come to me for reasons of stupefied hungers.
She reaches into the lingerie closet,
showing me my garter belts as if they were anorexic eels
from a starved sea. She tells me not to resuscitate.
She eats my garters like linguini.
She lights a cigarette and says her wings were ripped from her
after she murdered a woman she was assigned to protect
because that woman had boiled her lover,
a lobster that looked like a heart full of blood,
a lobster with blue blood who had given her so much;
the sound of his boiling body.
The cigarette has burned to an ash tower,
and the ashes drop off when she moves
to eat one of her arms.
Defeated, she lies there, beautifully bloodied
on the deathly pond of my wood-swirled floor,
her life leaping onto my windowsill.
I stand there, watching her give up.

# Nights Marred Like Crickets in Metal Fan Blades

I leave the cricket alone
and watch it die in metal fan blades.
All of you, my nightmares, have made me mean tonight,
you who have spliced
my conscious and subconscious barcodes together
into one black globule of ink.

I see one of you, nightmares, on the lawn;
even though it is morning and I am awake,
still I see you.
Your hands are on your hips.
I want to give you nothing.
Your gaze holds me like a handshake
as you tell me, in superimposed voices,
how to break myself into pieces,
how to use a revolver to shoot
the voicebox from a cricket.

The first time you came to me
I was in a room as small and dark as a nostril.
You squeezed my bare shoulder
as if it were a heart in need of a massage.
Was I alive yet? Or was I dead
and you stuck my heart in a brown paper bag
overnight? Are you able to bring me back?
I was alive the following night, evidently.
Your teeth soaking into my shoulder,
the juices lining you like vermouth
on a chilled glass.

The morning that followed,
the cricket sat in several pieces on my porch.
Something was bright about her,
as if some metal had remained on her

as if she had made some commitment to the metal
while she was in the biting blades of many deaths.
Her voice in pieces surrounded me as I walked out onto the porch:
Her voice like staples, or forceps.

## Rape Dreams

I am raped only by things, never people:
champagne flutes and cigarette lighters.
No, never a broomstick. Nothing obvious.
I am plagued by rapists I could never convict,
rapists who hide in kitchen cupboards, in the drawers of bureaus.
I believe I may have been born into a rebellion of inanimate objects.
I am never attacked on the street, even in darkness.
I am raped in daylight as I sleep.
I am put out with chloroform.
I resign myself to staying in an empty house,
just walls and floors, and I crave the wind, the sun and the moon.
When I go outside, I love the sky.
Someone must take me there—the sky the only place I can go,
the ultimate of nothing.
Space so cold; the sun, hot.
The moon's pockmarks the perfect cubby,
I need to go there, be there.

*But one night on a beach:*
*a boy with blonde hair,*
*who could run in the dark with the ocean's humming,*
*with the overwhelming beauty of the mystery of the sea,*
*the overwhelming beauty with the great potential for violence.*

The sky spits me out like a meteor, an exiled star.
I cover my ears, shut my mouth tight.
So much commanding me to fear it.

## My Libido

is in a downtown bar,
in a vintage Gucci dress
and purple Prada pumps—
the dress I had dreamed of owning:
black satin, three-quarter-length with ruffled neck,
sleeves and hemline. My libido walked away
from my table in innumerable frustrations,
the Gucci trailing her hips like satin soldiers,

a feminine, no nonsense female
who had been living it up in my heart,
using my sternum as her own personal bar,
drinking Cosmopolitans into the wee hours.

In retrospect, I know she tried to let me in on something,
something top secret that lives in all of us,
especially those who refuse the nonabstract,
possessing odd bloods and fleshes.

When she had first approached me,
the smoke from her cigarette framing her sacredly.
I asked, *Who are you?*
She showed me her world of Cosmopolitan-topped sternums,
and my own heart beating with steady flames and gasps;
my blood, veins and capillaries: her creeks, roads and alleyways.

Later she lay between me and the Other.
She lay there chain-smoking and waiting for my acceptance of her.
She entered my dreams and dropped hints,
hints that floated in formations trying for logic,
pleading for my understanding.
And she was real there and everywhere.
And as I looked at the emptiness around me,

I understood the roots of it all.
My libido, lying here with me and this Other:
medications and resulting frustrations the only tangibles.

In the morning after the Other left,
we took an aspirin and talked of the pixies
who had been ravaging my brain in the nights before her.
We both sat there, with Nescafé, revealed.
We became what we needed to be:
one entity in the machine of my pores.

## Philosophy in the Boudoir

*after Rene Magritte*

Philosophy, the lady in dark corners,
her lively toes peeking out of empty stilettos.

Lady, you hang in a wooden closet in a boudoir,
hoping for a philosophy of sex to come to you,
finally, after Kant, Heidegger, Sartre.

The philosophy of sex where a man needs you,
needs your lively toes that come from empty stilettos,
your perky breasts that sway from an empty hanging nightie.

I see you now and you speak in a voice, unrecognizable.
A voice that has resided in your lungs for centuries.
I will wait near you for everything.

I will wait near you and listen for you to finish
discussions and percussions, a philosophy of sex.
You, a woman hanging, breasts residing on the outside

of a pink nightie, toes, so lively now, empty stilettos.
You talk behind the wood of the boudoir closet,
whisper to yourself or anyone who will listen,

and you love the philosophy of sex. It comes to you.
Simply talking achieves a fruition, no physical contact.
Not yet. No one is around you as you hear others testing

theories you feel you have only just created.
Philosophy, you do not even have a head, a mind,
tangible ears, but you think, you hear,

you wait in the dark and feel lonely and so much else.
How is it you can do so much possessing so little?
You are an abstractness I love, and I love you.

But I do feel in competition. I wait near you,
outside the closet of the boudoir where you simply hang.
My moanings entertain and intrigue you, but it is you

who possesses the truth in this room. The man here,
nothing. You are not missing much in the execution.
You have the gentle luxury of nothing.

I open the closet, revealing you. My coat hangs near
you. My hands cup your breasts, Philosophy,
my thumb moves your heart over more to the right

like bending spines reaching for something
from the carpeted floors of boudoirs.

## Han Bellmer's Baby at Two

We are still ghosts to him
moving through the house
unnoticed. But I hope he loves us

in some way, in some inexact way.
The monumental things
are what Hans never notices—

a woman and his baby,
bouncing through life in his house
just barely. We are the saddest girls

this side of the street tonight.
I am practically certain he resents us,
yet how can he resent what he

does not see? We are, to Hans, things
in life that go unnoticed—
your daily flushes of the toilet,

your inhales and exhales.
There was even a day
when he almost sat on my baby,

when I screamed *stop* and pushed
him away. And he only continued
his descent into his brown bouclé chair.

The curtains were shoving the windows
out of the way as I stood in his face
and screamed that night, right into his face,

as loud and as shrill as I could be,
my daughter screamed right with me,
her eyes wet, wild, and showing signs

of being wronged, her cheeks red
as her little mouth, larynx.
He said nothing. Didn't move.

I picked up my daughter
and went into the kitchen.
I heated up the oven, 350 degrees

Fahrenheit, and placed in its center,
one sweet potato. It looked so tragic,
all alone in there, but it was all I knew

that night with screams and silence
dancing. I craved an autumn orange.

## Two Men in Sepia Came to Me

And two men in sepia come to me tonight
as you snore next to me. They enter
my brain through my ear slots.
How well the two of them blend in,
in their twilight camouflage.
Tonight, I chose to sleep naked, body and brain,
in expectation of them.

We eat imaginary lobster at an imagined banquet.
Rabbits multiply at my feet, but not by anyone else's.
I breast-feed a thousand newborns.
A line forms behind me, hungry.
I crave a gimlet.
Today has been long and threatens to be longer.
These men in sepia have brought me to a world
where daylight never ends, the light by which I feed rabbits.
My nipples now as round and red as plums.
I want to be in a world of wet.

I was pleased to make their acquaintance.

## So Nice to See You Again

That day outside the abattoir,
you were wringing the necks of chickens,
and their feathers smelled like fermented oysters.
I was still happy to see you,
though your eyes offended me:
two tiny cups of egg-drop soup.
Now I feel your eyes have been trying to tell me
what your mouth could not.

After you put the chickens down,
their necks wrung into featherless ropes,
your fingers looked like cigarette butts
smeared with red lipstick.
You walk to me on two legs, bowed and cautious,
legs that seem to be close cousins to the chicken necks.
When you were in front of me
you were as silent as a turtle.

You turned then,
to line up hooves against a wall,
arranging them into something meaningful.
Do you have a habit of arranging hooves?
A hobby when the days became so long?
If you sleep at night, are your eyelids able to close?
And if your eyelids close,
is there almost nothing for them to closet?

## Entering the Body of Mae West

I never knew you had four small chins,
stairsteps from your checkered-floor-chest.
Stairs to get to your mouth, those lips.
I walk up your chest,
admiring your drapery hair.
I want to go between your lips,
enter your mouth, enter you
to do some scientific research.
You are lovely, your eyes oversexed
but also persistent in the task of dying.
You look so lovely that I have remembered
how wonderful the word *lovely* is:
the way it tongues the teeth, the palate,
the way you will tongue my body
upon my entering
to do some scientific research.

When I put my foot on your first chin-step,
everything becomes cold:
the air made new by your breath.
You are cold and lovely,
Your lips, a soiled red, are the color of a lamp
with a chemise draped over its shade.
You who are the only one to tell us all
once and for all, the truth about beauty and anguish.
The beauty and anguish that create the loveliness in coldness.
We all must know the secret to pulling off pouty lips
while wearing chandelier earrings.

I apologize as I pry open your lips as if you were a choking child
and step on the cushion of your bottom lip.
You seem to approve of me
as you let me gaze into your opened mouth,

under your tongue at the frenulum;
your tongue then lies down again to reveal
your tongue, a Peruvian rug, silently and succinctly sewn.
I step upon it, shoeless.
You flick your tongue backward and I fall
down through your esophagus, a tarnished sterling silver,
and into your stomach.
My lab notebook asks forgiveness
for drawing a blank.
I awaken on a winter beach, my empty notebook nearby.
But here you are again, Mae, here we are, reflected
in the fan blades hovering above us,
in this world which is really a room.

## Elegy for Hans Bellmer

For you, today, I have removed my foot, my right foot,
and placed it lovingly in the coiled curls of my hair.

It will be Sunday soon and cakes will need to be made.
I am testing the balance of space and time.

The footing I will need to mix batters calms as it is terrifyingly calm.
But this I do for you, lovely one

who cleans the sink of my heart with scouring pads.

**Notes**

Hans Bellmer (1902-1975) was a surrealist artist known best for his doll creations that he referred to as *La Poupee*. In addition to these doll sculptures, he is also known as a surrealist photographer since he photographed his dolls and then deconstructed them to recycle the parts for new dolls.

The Dali paintings that appear in "Two Paintings by Salvador Dali" are *Apparition of Face and Fruit Dish on a Beach* and *Female Figure with Head of Flowers,* respectively.

The Rene Magritte painting referred to in "Philosophy in the Boudoir" is a painting by the same title.

photo by Daniel Lager

Carrie McGath received her B.A. in English from Ohio University and her Master of Fine Arts in poetry from Western Michigan University. She is currently working as a Librarian and lives in Kalamazoo, Michigan.

# New Issues Poetry

Vito Aiuto, *Self-Portrait as Jerry Quarry*

James Armstrong, *Monument in a Summer Hat*

Claire Bateman, *Clumsy; Leap*

Kevin Boyle, *A Home for Wayward Girls*

Michael Burkard, *Pennsylvania Collection Agency*

Christopher Bursk, *Ovid at Fifteen*

Anthony Butts, *Fifth Season; Little Low Heaven*

Kevin Cantwell, *Something Black in the Green Part of Your Eye*

Gladys Cardiff, *A Bare Unpainted Table*

Kevin Clark, *In the Evening of No Warning*

Cynie Cory, *American Girl*

Peter Covino, *Cut Off the Ears of Winter*

James D'Agostino, *Nude with* Anything

Jim Daniels, *Night with Drive-By Shooting Stars*

Joseph Featherstone, *Brace's Cove*

Lisa Fishman, *The Deep Heart's Core Is a Suitcase*

Robert Grunst, *The Smallest Bird in North America*

Paul Guest, *The Resurrection of the Body and the Ruin of the World*

Robert Haight, *Emergences and Spinner Falls*

Mark Halperin, *Time as Distance*

Myronn Hardy, *Approaching the Center*

Brian Henry, *Graft*

Edward Haworth Hoeppner, *Rain Through High Windows*

Cynthia Hogue, *Flux*

Joan Houlihan, *The Mending Worm*

Christine Hume, *Alaskaphrenia*

Josie Kearns, *New Numbers*

David Keplinger, *The Clearing; The Prayers of Others*

Maurice Kilwein Guevara, *Autobiography of So-and-So: Poems in Prose*

Ruth Ellen Kocher, *When the Moon Knows You're Wandering; One Girl Babylon*

Gerry LaFemina, *Window Facing Winter*

Steve Langan, *Freezing*

Lance Larsen, *Erasable Walls*

David Dodd Lee, *Abrupt Rural; Downsides of Fish Culture*
M.L. Liebler, *The Moon a Box*
Alexander Long, *Vigil*
Deanne Lundin, *The Ginseng Hunter's Notebook*
Barbara Maloutas, *In a Combination of Practices*
Joy Manesiotis, *They Sing to Her Bones*
Sarah Mangold, *Household Mechanics*
Gail Martin, *The Hourglass Heart*
David Marlatt, *A Hog Slaughtering Woman*
Louise Mathias, *Lark Apprentice*
Gretchen Mattox, *Buddha Box; Goodnight Architecture*
Lydia Melvin, *South of Here*
Carrie McGath, *Small Murders*
Paula McLain, *Less of Her; Stumble, Gorgeous*
Sarah Messer, *Bandit Letters*
Wayne Miller, *Only the Senses Sleep*
Malena Mörling, *Ocean Avenue*
Julie Moulds, *The Woman with a Cubed Head*
Marsha de la O, *Black Hope*
C. Mikal Oness, *Water Becomes Bone*
Bradley Paul, *The Obvious*
Katie Peterson, *This One Tree*
Elizabeth Powell, *The Republic of Self*
Margaret Rabb, *Granite Dives*
Rebecca Reynolds, *Daughter of the Hangnail; The Bovine Two-Step*
Martha Rhodes, *Perfect Disappearance*
Beth Roberts, *Brief Moral History in Blue*
John Rybicki, *Traveling at High Speeds* (expanded second edition)
Mary Ann Samyn, *Inside the Yellow Dress; Purr*
Ever Saskya, *The Porch is a Journey Different From the House*
Mark Scott, *Tactile Values*
Hugh Seidman, *Somebody Stand Up and Sing*
Martha Serpas, *Côte Blanche*
Diane Seuss-Brakeman, *It Blows You Hollow*
Elaine Sexton, *Sleuth*
Marc Sheehan, *Greatest Hits*
Heidi Lynn Staples, *Guess Can Gallop*
Phillip Sterling, *Mutual Shores*